8/20   9/21
11/19   34
34

PROJECT SCIENCE

WATER AND FLOATING

Alan Ward

Franklin Watts

New York • London • Toronto • Sydney

© 1992 Franklin Watts

Franklin Watts, Inc.
95 Madison Avenue
New York, NY 10016

Library of Congress Cataloging-in-Publication Data

Ward, Alan, 1932-
    Water and floating / by; Alan Ward.
        p. com. — (Project science)
    Includes index.
    Summary: Uses simple experiments and activities to demonstrate the
properties of water and such principles as floating.
    ISBN 0-531-14230-2
    1. Archimedes' principle — Juvenile literature. 2. Floating
bodies — Experiments — Juvenile literature. 3. Water — Juvenile
literature. 4. Water — Experiments — Juvenile literature.
[1. Water — Experiments. 2. Floating bodies — Experiments.
3. Experiments.] I. Title. II. Series: Ward, Alan, 1932-
Project science.
QC147.5.W37 1993
532'.2 — dc20

92-6260
CIP   AC

Series Editor: A. Patricia Sechi
Editor: Jane Walker
Design: Mike Snell
Illustrations: Alex Pang
Typesetting: Spectrum, London

Printed in Great Britain

CONTENTS

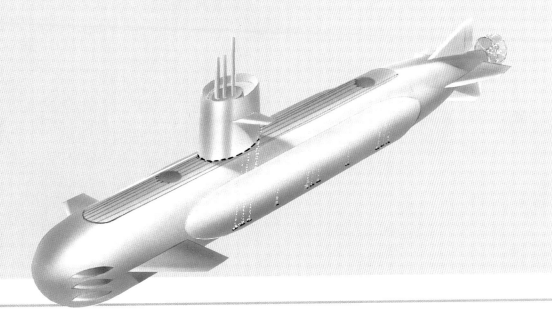

WATER AS A LIQUID

Water, like all other substances, is made of tiny invisible pieces called atoms and molecules. In a liquid, the atoms and molecules slide over each other. When you pour some water into a container with a flat surface, it spreads out to cover the bottom. All liquids will do this when poured into such a container.

How to make water look more...or less

Put some water in one of the jars and add a drop of food coloring. Now pour the water from jar to jar, trying not to spill any of it. See how the same amount of water changes shape in the different jars.

Does the amount of water sometimes look more?

Does the amount of water sometimes look less?

How do you know that the amount of water stays the same?

Gravity and water

The pull of gravity makes water spread out.

Fill two-thirds of the bottle with water and screw on the lid. Tilt the bottle in different directions and watch the level of the water in both the main part of the bottle and in its handle. What do you notice about the water level?

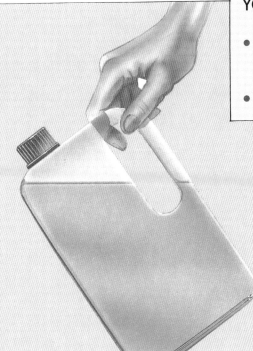

What has happened?
The water in the bottle finds its own level. This is because gravity is always pulling water down. Gravity makes water run downhill in streams and rivers. If you pour some water on the ground at the top of a slope in the playground, you can see it form into a winding river as gravity pulls it downward.

Did you know?
A special kind of well called an artesian well supplies water to fountains such as those of Trafalgar Square in London.

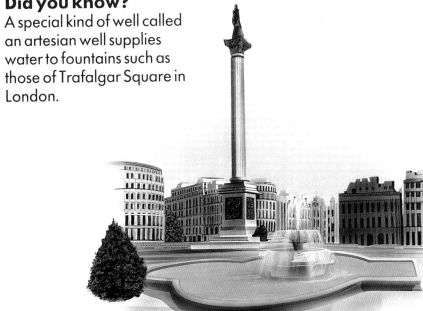

Sometimes the sides and bottom of a valley have layers of waterproof clay. The ground between two of these layers may hold water. Rain falls on the hills and becomes trapped between the layers, like a sandwich. If a well is bored into the valley, the trapped water spurts up. This is an artesian well. Gravity helps water to find its own level.

WATER AS A GAS

Gases can spread out in all directions.
When you blow up a balloon, the gases
in your breath spread out inside the
balloon to fill up the space inside.

Vanishing puddles

Heat energy from the sun
dries up puddles of rain,
turning the liquid water
into water vapor. This is
an invisible gas that goes
into the air.

When the sun comes out
after a summer rainstorm,
wait until the rain starts to
dry up and then find a
puddle. You need to find
a small shallow one on a
concrete surface. **Make
sure your puddle is
in a safe place.**

YOU NEED:

- chalk
- a watch

Use the chalk to draw
around the outside of the
puddle. Wait for 15
minutes and then draw
around the puddle again.
The second chalk line will
be inside the first one you
drew.

Keep chalking around the
puddle every 15 minutes
until the water dries up. Time
how long it takes for the
puddle to vanish.

Puddles vanish more quickly
when it is windy.

Puddles take longer to
vanish in winter sunshine.

Evaporation

The process of liquid water turning into a gas is called evaporation.

Tie the wet cloth to one end of the stick. Now hang the string in a doorway

and fix the stick so that it is dangling from the string. The stick should be in a horizontal position. As the cloth dries, the end of the stick becomes lighter and moves upward.

What has happened?

The water in the cloth starts to dry in the warm surroundings. It "boils away slowly," or evaporates, and turns into a gas called water vapor. When something dries, it loses water and so it weighs less. Dry laundry weighs less than wet laundry.

Condensation

The process of water vapor turning back into liquid water is called condensation. You can get water vapor from the air to condense and become a liquid.

Put the chilled can, unopened, on a table indoors. Wait a few minutes before touching the can. Does it feel wet?

Where do you think the wetness is coming from? The water vapor in the air cools when it touches the sides of the chilled can. It condenses on the can and becomes liquid water again.

Did you know?

When water is heated and boils, it becomes an invisible gas called steam. Another name for steam is water vapor.

The morning dew you see is formed when invisible water vapor from the air condenses on the cold ground, on grass and even on spiders' webs and makes visible drops of liquid water.

Did you know?

The steam that comes out of a kettle of boiling water is invisible. But it soon cools in the air and turns back into tiny droplets of liquid water. These form the whitish cloud that you see. Real clouds in the sky form like this. They, too, are made of droplets of liquid water, not gas or steam.

WATER AS A SOLID

When water freezes, a lot of the energy that makes its molecules vibrate, or shake, and slide over each other is removed. The molecules vibrate less and so they stay together as a solid lump — of ice.

YOU NEED:

- an ice cube from the freezer
- a plate

Put the ice cube on the plate. Take a close look at it, touch it, and taste it. Write down all the things you notice about the ice cube. Scientists always write down their observations.

What color is it?

Does it feel rough or smooth?

Can you see any bubbles inside it?

What does it taste like?

Does the ice smell?

Does the air around the ice cube feel chilly?

How long does it take to melt?

See what else can you find out and write down about your ice cube.

An ice competition

What can you do to stop ice from melting? Have a competition with your friends to see who can make their ice last the longest.

Wrap the ice cubes in the various materials. Put them in different places, but not in a refrigerator or freezer. You could try putting one in a thermos.

YOU NEED:

- ice cubes
- newspaper
- scraps of cloth
- aluminum foil
- other materials, such as plastic wrap, old socks, paper towels, etc.

An incredible ice balloon

Blow up the balloon and then let the air out. This will make the balloon stretchy. Now fill the balloon with water and tie a knot in its neck. Put the water-filled balloon in the dish and put the dish inside the freezer.

YOU NEED:

- a round balloon
- a dish
- water
- scissors

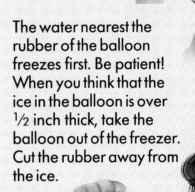

The water nearest the rubber of the balloon freezes first. Be patient! When you think that the ice in the balloon is over ½ inch thick, take the balloon out of the freezer. Cut the rubber away from the ice.

Use the scissors carefully to dig a small hole in the ice shell. You can then pour out the water that did not have time to freeze. You will have a most unusual "ice balloon." Think of a way to stop it from melting right away.

EXPERIMENTING WITH ICE

Ice magic

Here is a way to saw a block of ice in half, without splitting it.

First, ask an adult if you can use the freezer. Make a block of ice by filling the container with water and then freezing it.

Tie a piece of string around the middle of each brick. Tie one end of the wire to the string on the first brick, and tie the other end to the string on the second brick. Remove the container from the freezer and take out the block of ice.

Place the chairs in a cool place. It would be best to do this outdoors where falling bricks will not hurt anyone or do any damage. Push the backs of the two chairs together and carefully place the ice block on top of them.

Hang the wire, which is weighted with a brick at each end, over the middle of the ice block. You can watch the wire cut through the ice, but without slicing it in half.

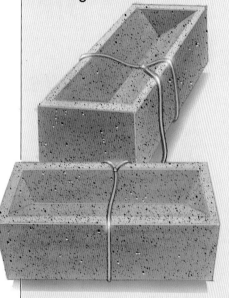

YOU NEED:

- a sandwich box
- water
- about 20 inches of strong thin wire
- string
- 2 chairs
- 2 house bricks

What has happened?

The wire squeezes its way down through the ice. We say that the wire is putting pressure on the ice. This pressure makes the ice melt so that the wire can move farther down. However, above the wire, where the pressure is reduced, the water refreezes and becomes ice again.

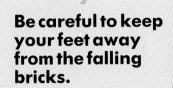

Be careful to keep your feet away from the falling bricks.

Did you know?

The pressure from an ice skater's skates melts the ice beneath. The skates slide easily in the wet grooves. After the skater has passed by, the water in the grooves refreezes.

CHANGING STATES OF WATER

All substances are made of matter, which is the mass of atoms and molecules found inside everything. Matter can exist in three forms, or states. The three ordinary states of matter are solids, liquids, and gases. Ice is the solid state of liquid water, and steam, or water vapor is its gaseous state.

These three states of matter can change into each other. But in order to change the state of a substance, heat energy must be either given or taken away. Heat energy melts ice to water and makes water boil away, or evaporate, into a gas called water vapor. When heat energy is removed, water vapor condenses into liquid water, and liquid water freezes into solid ice.

Melting ice

When heat energy is given to ice, the ice melts into liquid water.

Float the ice cube in the warm water. The bottom part of the ice melts quickly, making the top part top-heavy. Watch

YOU NEED:

- an ice cube
- a bowl of warm water

the ice as it rolls about before changing into a liquid and finally disappearing. The water has provided the heat needed to melt the ice.

Evaporating water

When heat energy is given to water, it changes into a gas.

Wet one of your wrists with cold water. It starts to feel cold. Your wrist feels cold until the water has dried up

and gone into the air as an invisible gas. Your body provided the heat needed to evaporate the cold water.

YOU NEED:

- cold water

Condensing water vapor

When heat energy is taken away from water vapor, it changes into a liquid.

Put the leaves in the bag and seal it with the closure tie. Put the bag on a sunny windowsill.

Leaves that are alive give out water vapor through tiny holes. The gas spreads out inside the bag. On the parts of the bag that are next to the outside air, where the bag is coldest, tiny drops of water will appear. The

water vapor has condensed to form water on the plastic. The outside air has taken away the heat, so that some of the water vapor in the bag has condensed.

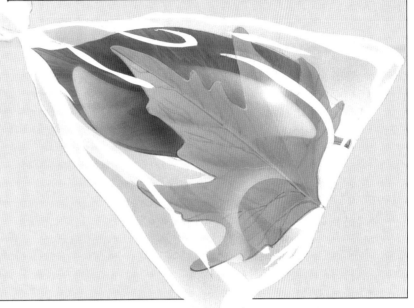

Freezing water

When heat is taken away from liquid water, it changes into solid ice.

Ask an adult for permission to use the freezer. Then, mix together the fruit juice and water. Pour the mixture into the spaces in the tray. Place a toothpick at an angle in each filled space. Put the tray in the freezer. In an hour or so, tasty fruit ice pops will be ready. The freezer takes heat away from the water in the fruit mixture so that it freezes.

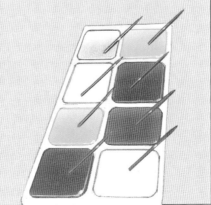

Did you know?

The three ordinary states of water can all be found in the weather. Snow and ice are really solid water, misty clouds and rain are liquid water, and humidity is water vapor in the air or the gaseous state of water.

WHAT IS DENSITY?

Ice cubes float in your glass of lemonade. Icebergs, which are really huge islands of ice, float in the sea. So ice, or frozen water, must weigh less than liquid water.

Every substance has something we call density, which has a similar meaning to "thickness." The more that the mass of atoms and molecules in a substance are packed into a space, then the denser that substance will be.

Bursting a bottle

See what happens if you fill a plastic bottle with water and allow the water to freeze.

Ask an adult for permission to use the freezer before you start. Fill the bottle with water and screw on the lid. Put the bottle in the dish and place the dish in the freezer. Leave it in the freezer overnight. In the morning you will see that the cap has burst.

YOU NEED:

- an empty plastic bottle with a screw-top lid
- water
- a dish

What has happened?

When water freezes, its molecules change their shape and take up more space. Ice weighs less than the same quantity of water. We say that the ice is less dense than water. A bucket of ice has fewer molecules than the same-sized bucket filled with liquid water.

Did you know?

When ice forms inside water pipes, it can split them. When the ice melts, water spills out of the burst pipe. That's when you need to call for the services of a plumber!

An underwater volcano

Water expands when it is heated. The water molecules vibrate more and more quickly and so they need more space to move about in. Hot water is not as dense as cold water. The molecules in cold water are more closely packed together and take up less space.

Fill the tank with cold water. Put a drop of food coloring into the jar and fill it to the brim with hot water. Ask an adult to help you do this. Use hot water from the sink—it does not need to be boiling.

Place the paper over the top of the jar and secure it with the rubber band. Stand the jar underwater at one end of the tank. Use the pencil to puncture two holes in the paper cover.

The hot colored water starts to rise up into the cold water. What you see is something like an underwater volcano. The warm colored water then spreads all over the surface. To see your volcano more clearly, hang a sheet of white paper behind the tank.

What do you think would happen if you floated some ice cubes at the other end of the tank? Try doing this and see if you were right.

WHY DO SOME OBJECTS FLOAT?

An object floats when water can push up on it with enough force to stop it from sinking. The pull of gravity that gives an object its weight makes it sink. As it sinks, the object pushes away water. The amount of water pushed away tries to push back on the object with the force of its own weight.

This push-up force is called upthrust. If the upthrust is equal to or greater than the weight of the object, then the object will float.

YOU NEED:

- a small plastic bag
- a bowl of water
- food coloring

Put some water in the bag and add a drop of food coloring. Fasten the bag. Place the bag of water in the bowl of water. It will float like a boat. Nearly all of its weight is its cargo of water. Notice the level of the water in the bag and in the bowl.

What has happened?
The water levels inside and outside the bag are equal. The bag must be pushing away its own weight of water. The upthrust of this pushed-away water keeps your bag "boat" afloat. We say that the water that is pushed away has been displaced.

Displacing water

If you try to float a solid lump of modeling clay in a bowl of water, it sinks. The modeling clay is denser than the water — it has more mass than the same amount of water. See what happens if you shape the clay into a boat and then try to float it.

Shape the clay into a boat that will float in the bowl of water. The boat's hollow shape displaces enough water to give the boat the upthrust it needs to stay afloat. Try adding marbles to your clay boat. You could have a competition with your friends to see whose boat will hold the most marbles without sinking. Make sure you all start with the same amount of modeling clay.

Floating and sinking

A solid lump of material that is denser than water will sink. Any material that is less dense than water will float. An object that floats is pulled down into the water by gravity. When the object has displaced enough water to get an upthrust that equals its own weight, the object will float.

Did you know?

Steel is about eight times more dense than water, yet huge oceangoing ships are made of steel. So how do they float? The steel is shaped into a shell-like hull that can displace an enormous amount of water. In fact, a ship's weight is given as its displacement of water, which is measured in tons.

FUN WITH FLOATERS

Superfloaters

Styrofoam is a soft and lightweight material. It is used for packing fragile objects, and styrofoam floats are used by people who are learning to swim.

Float the styrofoam in the water. Its density is much lower than the density of water. Although the block of styrofoam is large, it weighs so little that it only has to displace a small amount of water to get enough upthrust to float.

See how much mass is needed to sink the styrofoam. You could place some coins or pebbles on the block, until it sinks. Then find out the weight of the coins.

A bottle submarine

Find out how you can make a bottle float and sink like a submarine.

Push one end of the tubing right down to the bottom of the bottle. Attach the tubing to the neck of the bottle with the rubber band. Sink the bottle in the bowl by filling it with water.

Blow gently into the free end of the tubing. See if you can get the bottom of the bottle to float up to the surface.

When the bottle just floats, squeeze the tubing to stop the air from escaping. To make the bottle sink again, stop squeezing the tubing. Now your bottle will float and sink, just like a real submarine.

YOU NEED:

- an empty bottle
- a length of rubber tubing (about ¼ inch in diameter)
- a small rubber band
- a deep bowl of water

What has happened?

Glass is denser than water, but a glass bottle floats because it is hollow, like a boat. When the glass bottle is filled with water, it sinks. But when you blow down the tubing, some of the water in the bottle is forced out and replaced by air, so the bottle floats up to the surface. When the air is let out through the tubing, the water refills the bottle and it sinks again.

Did you know?

A submarine is fitted with special water tanks called ballast tanks. Water is pumped in and out of these tanks to make the submarine sink (submerge) or float.

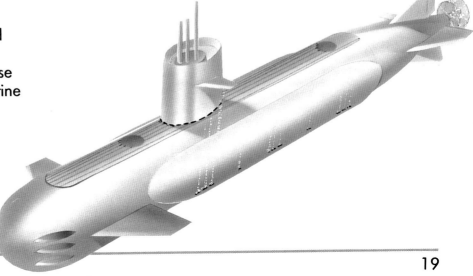

TESTING EGGS IN WATER

In an open-air market in Africa, an egg merchant sits on a carpet. Beside her is a pile of eggs and a bowl of water. Before you buy an egg, you must first test it in the water. Do you know why? You do the test to find out whether the egg is fresh or not.

A fresh egg will sink in the water. It is denser than water. A fresh egg has more mass than the amount of water that it can displace. A bad egg floats because it is less dense than water. It has become rotten and dried up. The insides have turned into a gas which escapes through tiny holes in the egg's shell. The bad egg can displace more than its own weight of water. The force of this water provides the upthrust that keeps the bad egg afloat.

Bad eggs

Use this test to find out how long it takes for a fresh egg to turn bad.

You also need lots of patience for this test. Don't store the egg in the refrigerator. Test the egg every day by placing it in the bowl of water. See how many days it takes for the egg to go bad.

When your test shows that the egg has gone bad, take it outdoors and break it. It will smell bad because it has spoiled.

YOU NEED:

- a fresh egg
- a bowl of tap water

An amazing egg trick

First, make some salty water by adding salt, a little at a time, to warm water in a saucepan. Keep stirring the water. Stop adding salt when no more will dissolve. A fresh egg should float in this salty mixture.

Half fill the jar with the salty water. Then fill the pitcher with fresh water and pour this on top of the salty water, without letting the waters mix. To do this, tilt the jar while you slowly pour in the fresh water.

Stop pouring when the jar is not quite full. Put it down and gently drop in your egg. The egg sinks in the fresh water and then bounces on the salty water and stops halfway down in the jar.

What has happened?

Salty water is denser than ordinary water. Because the fresh water has a lower density, it floats in a thick layer on top of the salty water. The fresh egg is denser than the ordinary water but less dense than the salty water, so it floats on top of the layer of salty water.

Did you know?

The Dead Sea in Israel is so salty that you can easily float on your back, while reading your favorite book.

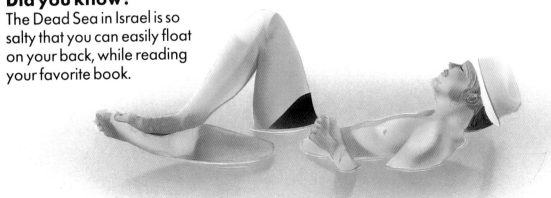

WATER PRESSURE

As a diver goes deeper and deeper down into the sea, more and more water directly above pushes down on the diver's body. The water presses down because it has weight. The deeper the diver goes, the more this force increases. This increasing force is called water pressure.

Testing water pressure

You can check whether water pressure increases with depth by doing these two tests.

Ask an adult to bore three holes in the side of the plastic bottle. Cover the holes with a strip of tape. Fill the bottle with water and stand it on the stool. You should do this trick outdoors, as it's a bit messy.

Hold the bottle firmly and tear off the strip of tape. Watch the water being driven out by pressure. Compare the distances covered by the three jets of water. See which jet of water reaches the farthest from the bottle.

YOU NEED:

- an empty plastic bottle
- tape
- a tall stool
- water

Did you know?

The body, or hull of a submarine has to be built with thick, strong walls. This is to stop the submarine from being crushed by water pressure when it dives very deeply in the sea.

Upward and downward

Water pressure acts upward as well as downward.

Ask an adult to remove both ends of the soup can, safely, and wash it so that you have a clean metal tube. Modern can openers do not leave sharp edges, but still be very careful when you handle your tube.

Hold the lid on the bottom of the tube while you lower it into the bowl until it is halfway underwater.

Carefully take your hand away from the lid. Notice what happens to it. Wait a few minutes and see what else happens to the lid.

What has happened?

The water pressure acts upward to stop the lid from sinking when you take your hand away from it. Gradually, water leaks under the lid and the water level inside the tube rises.

When the water level inside the tube is the same as that outside, the lid finally sinks. Do you think that the water pressure on each side of the lid has to be equal before the lid will sink?

For the second test, the tubing should be longer than the height of the jar. Ask an adult to make three holes in the tubing. Fill the jar with water and place the tube in the jar so that the holes are covered by water. Start blowing gently into the tubing.

You should be able to make air bubbles come out of the holes. You are blowing against the pressure of the water. You will need to blow hardest to make air come out of the bottom hole.

From what you have observed in these two tests, you can see that water pressure increases with depth.

FUN WITH PRESSURE

A diver in a bottle

Partly open one of the paper clips and push it up inside the pen cap so that its top half is wedged tightly inside the cap. Hang the second paper clip from the wedged one. This is your pen-cap diver.

Test your pen cap by floating it in water. It should only just be able to float. If it floats too well, replace the second paper clip with a heavier or larger one.

Fill the bottle to the brim with water. Float the pen cap in the water. Screw on the bottle cap, trapping as little air as possible between the cap and the top of the water. Now squeeze the bottle and watch your pen-cap diver go down. Notice what happens when you stop squeezing the bottle.

What has happened?
When you squeeze the bottle, you create pressure that forces more water inside the pen cap. The bubble of air inside the cap is squeezed into a smaller space. This makes your diver more dense, so it sinks.

When you stop squeezing the bottle, the pressure is reduced and the bubble of air trapped inside the pen cap can spread out again. This drives out some of the water, making the diver less dense and able to float.

How does a siphon work?

Sometimes water can be forced to flow uphill, without having to be pumped. The driving force that does this is water pressure, and this movement of water is called siphon action.

Fill one of the bottles almost to the top. Dip one end of the tubing in this bottle. Carefully suck the other end of the tubing until it is almost full of water. Remove it from your mouth and put your thumb over the end. **Don't let any water run back down the tubing.**

Hold the bottle with the water up to your shoulder level. Poke the free end of tubing into the second bottle, taking your thumb off the end as you do this. Water immediately starts to flow from the first bottle to the second bottle. It stops flowing when the water levels in the two bottles are the same. You have made a siphon.

By alternately raising first one bottle, and then the other, you can make the

water in your siphon flow backward and forward. Water pressure is the siphon's driving force.

Did you know?
You can use a siphon to empty water from a fish tank. Fill a tube with water. Put a thumb over each end and lower one end into the tank. Put the other end in the bucket. Notice how the water flows uphill from the fish tank and down into a bucket or container held below the tank.

WHAT IS SURFACE TENSION?

Water, like other liquids, behaves as if it has a tight skin stretched across its surface. But the skin isn't a real one. This idea is called surface tension. The word "tension" means tightness.

Coins in water

Fill the glass up to the brim with water. Try not to wet the sides of the glass. Carefully drop a nickel in the water. The coin sinks to the bottom, but the water does not overflow. The water acts as if it has a skin, and its surface bulges when you put in the nickel.

Now put in more coins and watch the surface of the water swell.

YOU NEED:

- a glass of water
- a pile of nickels

YOU NEED:

- a glass
- a pitcher of water
- a Ping Pong ball

The floating ball

Place the glass on a level table and fill it to the brim with water. Try to float the ball in the middle of the glass. Ask your friends to have a try. None of you will be able to do it.

Pour in a little more water and see how the water's invisible skin makes this trick work.

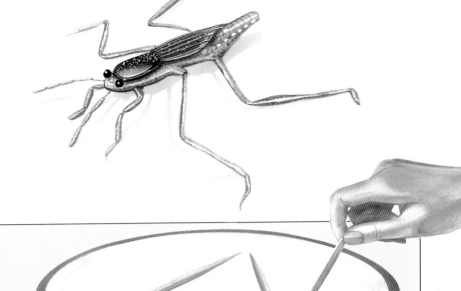

Did you know?

Insects called pond skaters and water striders live and feed on the skinlike surface of water. Look for them on the surface of ponds and streams. They do not float in the usual way. The surface tension holds them up, so they do not sink.

YOU NEED:

- 4 wooden toothpicks
- some dishwashing liquid
- a shallow baking tray or large plate
- water

Floating sticks

Pour some water onto the tray or plate and float three of the toothpicks in the water. Use the fourth toothpick to push the other three into the shape of a triangle.

Put a drop of dishwashing liquid on the end of your finger. Now touch the middle of the triangle with this finger. Presto! The sticks fly apart.

What has happened?

The dishwashing liquid has weakened the surface of the water. The surface tension of the water outside the triangle pulls the three toothpicks apart.

Did you know?

Normally a coin will sink to the bottom of a glass of water because it is denser than the water. But some small metal coins can be made to rest on the surface, like a pond skater. Here's a way of lowering a steel needle onto the surface of a glass of water so that it doesn't sink.

Bend the ends of a hairpin. Place the needle so that it rests on the hooked ends. Now lower the needle into the water.

In order for these experiments to be successful, make sure that everything you use, including your hands, is clean.

EXTRA PROJECTS

Invisible spaces

Even when a glass is full of water, there are still empty spaces between the molecules of water.

Fill the glass to the brim with water. Very carefully, put small wads of cotton ball into the water. You should be able to make the cotton balls fill up every part of the glass without spilling any water.

Standing on water

Here's a challenge for your friends. Ask if anyone can float seven corks upright in a bowl of water. It's impossible to do this with separate corks! When they have all failed, you can show them how it's done.

Hold the corks upright in a bundle. Form them into a neat raft, shaped like a flower or similar. Keep holding them in this shape while you dip the bundle of corks underwater. Then bring them up to the surface and take away your hand. You may need to practice a few times before doing this in front of your friends.

What has happened?

The surface tension of the water helps to stick the corks together, so that you can float them all upright as if they were a single cork.

Did you know?

The body of an adult produces enough heat every day to boil 30 quarts of freezing cold water.

Chilly challenges

See if you can make some of these unusual ice shapes.

Make a block of ice shaped like a hand. (You will need something to help you shape the ice.)

Make a block of ice with a small plastic toy hidden inside it.

Make a block of ice shaped like a doughnut. (A heavy can placed inside a round dish might help.)

Little iceberg

Icebergs are a serious danger to ships at sea. Do you know just how big an iceberg really is?

YOU NEED:

- an ice cube
- a glass of water

Float the ice in the glass of water. The ice cube is a miniature iceberg. By looking at your ice cube, try and imagine how much of the ice from a real iceberg is hidden under the sea.

GLOSSARY

A

atom
The smallest piece of any one of the basic substances or elements.

C

condensation
When a gas cools and turns into a liquid.

D

density
The amount of mass which occupies a certain space.

dew
Wetness on the ground outside from water vapor which has changed into liquid water.

displacement
The amount of water that an object can push away.

droplet
A tiny drop of liquid which is only just visible.

E

evaporation
When a liquid is heated and turns into a gas.

F

flotation
When a liquid pushes up on an object with enough force to stop it from sinking.

freezing
When a liquid changes its state and turns into a solid.

G

gas
The state of matter where a substance spreads in all directions to fill the available space.

gravity
The pull of the earth which attracts all solids, liquids, and gases toward the earth's surface.

H

heat energy
A form of energy that can change the state of matter of a solid, liquid, or gas. Heat energy can be given to, or taken away from, a substance.

L

liquid
The state of matter where a substance is in a watery form.

M

molecule
A very small piece of any substance which is made when two or more atoms join together.

P

pressure
The force that presses down on a certain area or surface.

S

siphon
A device that can move a liquid upward, without pumping it.

solid
The state of matter where a substance is in the form of a fixed shape or lump.

state of matter
One of the three different forms (solid, liquid, or gas) of any substance.

steam
Water in the state of a gas. Another name for steam is water vapor.

surface tension
When molecules cling tightly together at the surface of a liquid and produce an effect like a skin.

U

upthrust
When the force of a liquid acts in an upward direction. Another name for upthrust is buoyancy.

V

vibrate
To shake or ripple in a regular way.

volcano
A hole in the earth's surface through which fire, melted rocks, steam, and hot ashes pour out.

W

water pressure
The force of water pressing down on an object.

water vapor
Water in the state of a gas. Another name for water vapor is steam.

INDEX